IN
THE
Hands
OF
THE
Potter

IN
THE

OF
THE

CAMILLE FRONK

DESERET
BOOK

SALT LAKE CITY, UTAH

Appreciation is expressed to Brian Christensen, who created most of the pottery and took the majority of photographs shown in this book. All images have been used with permission.

Visit us at deseretbook.com

Library of Congress Cataloging-in-Publication Data

Fronk, Camille.
  In the hands of the Potter / Camille Fronk.
      p.   cm.
  Includes bibliographical references and index.
  ISBN 1-59038-089-4 (alk. paper)
  1. Spiritual life—Church of Jesus Christ of Latter-day Saints.
  2. Church of Jesus Christ of Latter-day Saints—Doctrines.   3. Samaritan woman (Biblical figure)   4. Spiritual life—Biblical teaching.   I. Title.
  BX8656.F76 2003
  248.4'89332—dc22   2003018243

Printed in the United States of America   72076
Publishers Printing, Salt Lake City, UT

10   9   8   7   6   5   4   3   2

To

J. Wayne and Roberta Harris Fronk,
for the blessing of life

Rob, Jayne, Jill, Thom, and Hal,
for the courage to explore life

Paul,
for the rediscovery of life

CONTENTS

ONE . . . 1

Discovering the Potter

TWO . . . 14

"We Are the Clay"

THREE . . . 27

Preparing the Clay

FOUR . . . 47

Centering the Clay

CONTENTS

FIVE . . . 55

Shaping the Vessel

SIX . . . 64

Entrusting Ourselves to the Potter

SEVEN . . . 78

The Completed Vessel

WORKS CITED . . . 87

ONE

Discovering the Potter

Finding God is a personal journey. No one can travel that path for us. While it is motivating and inspiring to hear another's witness of discovery, souvenir snapshots are nothing compared to being there.

In the parable of the ten virgins, Christ taught that things of the Spirit are not directly transferable; the testimony of a family member or friend will never suffice. We must each "buy for [our]selves" (Matthew 25:9) the precious preparation that invites God's all-powerful transformation. If our characters will ever be molded and shaped to mirror the Savior's, sometime, someway, somewhere we must discover for ourselves the power of His infinite atonement. Only when we strive to "work out [our] own salvation with fear and trembling"

(Philippians 2:12) will we find that Christ died and lived again for each one of us. Only when we "walk by faith, not by sight" (2 Corinthians 5:7) do we comprehend that He is our *personal* Savior.

Walking by faith does not promise a life free from difficulty. On the contrary, opposition is a frequent traveling companion, tempting us to cancel the trip or search for an alternative route. But there is only one route to God. He is the way. Jesus did not teach, "I am *a* way." He taught, "I am *the* way" (John 14:6; emphasis added).

Sariah, mother to Book of Mormon prophet Nephi, discovered that solitary Way. Only when faced by her greatest fear—the loss of all four of her sons—did she realize that her prophet-husband's testimony did not suffice. Sariah had to know for herself. With a mother's premonition that her sons were in danger, and recognizing that none could help but God, Sariah turned wholeheartedly to Him, and in turn discovered His will for her and her family. With her sons safely returned, Sariah testified, "*Now I know of a surety* that the Lord hath commanded my husband to flee into the wilderness; . . . and . . . protected my sons . . . and given them power whereby they could accomplish the thing which the Lord hath commanded them" (1 Nephi 5:8; emphasis added). Finding God unleashed untapped strength in Sariah; she is never reported to have murmured again.

In this precarious world, fed by perpetual information explosions and high-speed access to life, we can temporarily fool ourselves into thinking we can find Him without ever leaving our comfort zones. Seeking to cover our vulnerability, we may settle for hanging out with the crowd on the road called "Status Quo." But God did not send us here to simply subsist. He sent us to walk by faith, to develop unshakable trust in Him, to make Him first in our lives, to live abundantly. God wants us to become like Him.

This book is about finding God oneself—a personal journey that can only be traveled alone—and His sweet tutelage and enabling power that sees us safely there.

I have not always trusted Christ's personal invitation

to "come unto me" (Matthew 11:28). I was a shy adolescent who wanted to do well without expending much effort. A series of experiences in my childhood and youth, however, charted my personal journey to find Christ's message for me.

The first time I was required to read scripture on my own was in ninth-grade seminary where the course of study was the Book of Mormon. Since I perceived that girls were not expected to really understand the text, I concluded that a cursory reading would suffice. I chose to satisfy the reading requirement by following along in my scriptures with my family's set of Book of Mormon recordings. These multiple records featured a man reading the text very slowly in a deep voice, void of variation or hint of emotion.

Seeking to expedite the "study" session, I increased the phonograph speed from 33 rpm to 78 rpm, which changed the sound of the man's voice to resemble an animated chipmunk but was still perfectly understandable. Finally, to increase interest, I created a form of competition where I sought to read the assigned text faster than the chipmunk. I always won. In this way, I confidently reported to my seminary teacher at the end of the school year that I had read the entire Book of Mormon.

In other ways, however, I received ideas in my youth that contradicted my assumptions that studying and professing religion were to be avoided.

The setting for most of my formal religious instruction was in the Latter-day Saint meetinghouse I attended throughout my youth—the Tremonton, Utah, First Ward. The 1928-built chapel features a large, bas-relief mural that fills the entire front wall behind the podium. The mural depicts the story from John 4 of a Samaritan woman who came to know Jesus and his mercy at a well. I stared at that mural every Sunday during worship services, and mid-week during Primary or mutual meetings. I often wondered what that woman had done to deserve such a prestigious place in our chapel. While I had never consciously studied the scriptural story, repeatedly seeing the scene of Jesus giving full attention in His teachings to a woman subliminally recorded an impression that Jesus found women capable of understanding His teachings. I began longing to be like that woman. I wanted Jesus to teach me, too.

Two defining experiences in that meetinghouse are particularly memorable. The first occurred when I was a "Firelight," the Primary class for ten-year-old girls. Our class of three girls was assigned the bishop's office, located right off the chapel, as our classroom. With our teacher, Mary Beth Neiderhauser, we sat in a small circle cradling our personal copies of the New Testament in our laps. The teacher gave each of us a red pencil, a bookplate, and a card-stock bookmark featuring a blond little girl reading her scriptures. Each week Sister Neiderhauser instructed us to mark a particular verse of scripture, using our bookmark as a straight edge, while she explained the passage to us.

One week our class scripture was from the New Testament. Something different happened inside me that day. Unexpectedly, I discovered that I understood the meaning of Christ's words. In that moment, I felt as though Jesus were teaching *me* at the well. After our class discussed what the verses meant, I returned to the New Testament text to note that Jesus said it far better than our explanation reflected. His words included a depth of meaning that our paraphrasing had missed. As I walked home from Primary that day, swinging my drawstring scripture bag in dramatic arches, I celebrated the fact that through His scriptures, the Savior had actually spoken to me!

The second realigning experience began during my junior year in high school. I was attending a regional youth fireside, held in my Tremonton First Ward chapel. The speaker was a woman from outside the region whose name probably never registered with me. Her remarks included a challenge for each of us to commit to read the Book of Mormon on our own, one page every day, until completion. My initial thought was, "I've already read it; I don't need to read it again." Of course I was referring to my chipmunk race two years before. Then suddenly I felt an inner desire to read it carefully this time, not for credit or public notice, but solely for my own understanding.

Torleif Knaphus's bas relief of the Savior with the woman at the well hangs on the wall at the Tremonton First Ward Chapel

Behind the speaker, I saw the mural of Jesus Christ desiring to help a woman to understand. How would I learn what He yearned to teach me if I never studied the scriptures? Now here I was being invited to raise my hand in commitment to read and ponder each page of the Book of Mormon. Indirectly, I felt the Savior issue me the same invitation as though He were facing me instead of the woman at the well. My hand went up.

Of course this second encounter with the Book of Mormon proved superior to my first experience. At times I was so drawn into the narrative that I forgot to stop at my single-page requirement. Often I felt a power that superceded the drama of any particular story. I began to make connections in God's plan of happiness for everyone who comes to earth. I had been taught about His plan in family home evenings, seminary, and at church, but pondering the Book of Mormon page by page led me to know that the plan was real, and that only God had the power to make it happen. I thought about what I would report to Jesus Christ at the time of the final judgment and how much I wanted to please

Him. And for the first time, I began to believe that within that great plan, God had a custom-made plan just for me. I began to wonder: What has He sent me to earth to do?

That was the question I asked God as frequently as any other. As I saw my life follow a path so foreign to what I expected, I often wondered if I had made a wrong turn. But phrases in my patriarchal blessing and evidence of small successes that were beyond my natural ability reinforced to me that God was molding me to become what only He could imagine.

Old Testament prophets used a metaphor of the Potter and the clay to illustrate God's preparation of each of us for our divine missions. Isaiah exclaimed, "But now, O Lord, thou art our father; we are the clay, and thou our potter; and we are the work of thy hand" (Isaiah 64:8). Elder Bruce R. McConkie explained how the Potter in the metaphor is a type of Jesus Christ, "meaning that he governs in the affairs of men so as to mould and shape earthen human vessels into vessels of honor and service to him" (*Mormon Doctrine*, 580).

As I have come to understand far more about the woman at the well, I realize that she was the least likely candidate to recognize the mortal Jesus as the long-awaited Messiah. But the Potter had been at work. He prepared her not only for that moment of encounter at her well, but also for her subsequent influence among her Samaritan villagers. The account of her transformation into a vessel of honor and service transcends both time and place. That is why her story has power to inspire many more than a little Mormon girl in Tremonton, Utah. Her scriptural story is a perfect illustration of the magnificent power manifest in the Potter as He prepares and shapes each unique lump of clay.

Shortly after joining the faculty at Brigham Young University, I visited Brian Christensen, a ceramics professor at the University. I wanted to know how a lump of clay is transformed into a work of art. In about an hour, Professor Christensen highlighted the process, opening my mind to greater lessons about Christ as the Potter and our potential when we trust in Him. I am indebted to him for leading me to see connections in our own journey to find God.

In this book, I suggest a parallel with the Samaritan woman's journey to come unto Christ and the remarkable process a Potter follows to form a perfected clay vessel. My hope is that such a study and example may prompt discoveries in the reader's personal journey to the Savior, reminders of the role the Master Potter has already performed in the reader's life. By design, this book is short. It can never be a substitute for uncovering the truths about the Potter from His source—the scriptures—but it may be a means to the supernal personal discovery that each life has a unique purpose, that God is in control, and that He will direct our paths.

TWO

"We Are the Clay"

As one of a million natural resources in the earth, unworked clay is not considered to be particularly valuable. It is readily available and holds no visible attraction. But this unpretentious raw material is one of God's creations. As such, even this lowly substance is capable of being formed into innumerable vessels, each having special purpose and unique worth. How appropriate to compare our mortal bodies to tabernacles of clay (see Mosiah 3:5). The comparison reminds us of our own nothingness, without the vision, skills, and sacrifice of the Master Potter.

Much like raw clay, the woman who met Jesus at the well would have been considered among the lowliest people in society for three major reasons. First, she

Raw, unworked clay reminds us of our own nothingness without the vision, skills, and sacrifice of the Master Potter.

PHOTO BY BRIAN CHRISTENSEN

was a Samaritan. At the time of Christ, the well where she encountered the Savior was located in a region inhabited by Samaritans, a people who had a nearly one-thousand-year history of contention with the Jews. Samaria is just north of Judea and south of Galilee. The Samaritan territory was the land inheritance given to the two tribes of Joseph (Ephraim and Manasseh) when the children of Israel first conquered the land. Centuries before the Samaritan woman met Jesus at the well, Joshua established the region as the first religious center for the Israelite nation. Mt. Ebal to the north, and Mt. Gerizim to the south, border the area.

Jacob's well is located near the foot of Mt. Gerizim, not far from the modern Palestinian city of Nablus. In New Testament times, the closest village was called Sychar, known in the Old Testament as Shechem. Here Jacob purchased land shortly after his favorable reunion with Esau, thereby giving the well its name.

Samaritans were viewed as ritually unclean by the Jews because of their tainted lineage. They were descended from a residue of the northern tribes, who were not deported during the Assyrian invasion of 722 B.C., and from foreign colonists introduced to the land of Israel by the conquering Assyrians from other parts of their expanding empire.

The Jewish Mishnah (a collection of oral traditions and rabbinic teachings about the Torah) warns: "He that eats the bread of the Samaritans is like to one that eats the flesh of swine" (Shebiith 8:10). The Jews, therefore, rejected the Samaritans' offer to assist them in reconstructing their temple. In retaliation, the Samaritans created obstacles that temporarily halted Jewish reconstruction. Finally, in 128 B.C., the Jewish high priest destroyed the Samaritan temple on Mt. Gerizim. In the days of Jesus, this enduring animosity between the Jews and the Samaritans encouraged most Jews to take an alternate route via the Jordan River Valley when traveling to Galilee from Jerusalem. By skirting the province of Samaria, Jews could avoid contact with the Samaritan people.

Secondly, the Samaritan woman would have been disregarded because she was a woman. The Mishnah

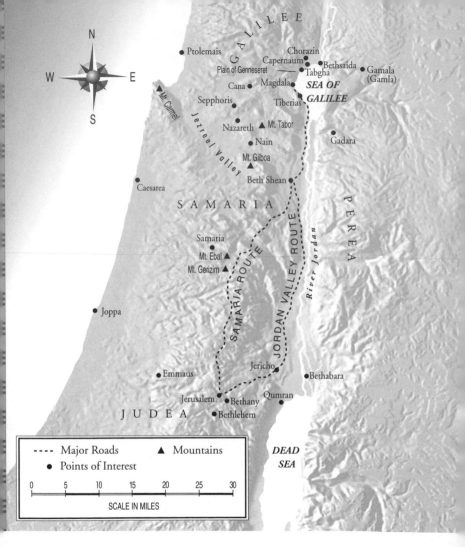

Jews traveling from Galilee to Judea could use two routes: one through Samaria, the other along the Jordan River Valley. The latter route was almost always the preferred choice.

MAP BY TOM CHILD

labels Samaritan women as "menstruants from their cradle," thereby making them regularly unclean (Niddah 4:1–3). Additionally, rabbinic literature warned Jewish men against public association with women, including their own wives. "He that talks much with womankind," the Mishnah reads, "brings evil upon himself and neglects the study of the Law and at the last will inherit Gehenna" (Aboth 1:5), meaning they qualify for everlasting burning in hell.

Not surprisingly, women were expected to do much of society's demanding, routine labor. For example, every day, either in the morning or evening (or both morning and evening), women went to the well to fetch water for their homes and families. Each woman walked the distance carrying a lengthy rope and a leather or animal-skin vessel. Jacob's well, where the Samaritan drew water daily, reportedly over 100 feet deep and 7 feet wide, is located some distance from the village of Sychar. After manually drawing water from the well, the woman would carry her rope and now-heavy waterpot back to her home, only to repeat the chore the next day. These and other perceptions led Jewish men to generally rank women lowest in their society.

Finally, this Samaritan woman would have been an outcast from society because she had not lived a chaste life. Scripture explains that she was previously married to five different men and was currently living with a man who was not her husband (see John 4:18). Consequently, both the Jews and her own people would have ostracized her. Perhaps this was the reason she came to the well during the "sixth hour," meaning six hours after sunrise, about noon. The increased heat at mid-day would have only added discomfort to her rigorous chore of fetching water. Did the woman choose this unusual hour because it was the least likely time to meet other women? If men showed their disdain by ignoring her, women could be even more vicious with their judgmental gazes and whispers intended to be heard.

The story of the woman at the well also tells us much about the Potter. Jesus was a Jew living in a culture that discouraged public communication with women. Yet we find him at the public well, deep in theological discussion with a clearly imperfect woman. Why? And why her?

In his *Lectures on Faith*, Joseph Smith identified several attributes of God, including that He is "no respecter of persons: but in every nation he that fears God and works righteousness is accepted of him" (3:17). This woman's lineage and lifestyle did not preclude her from receiving the Lord's greatest promises. Additionally, the Prophet Joseph taught that God (the Potter) "changes not, neither is there variableness with him" (*Lectures*, 3:15); "he was God before the world was created, and the same God . . . after it was created" (*Lectures*, 3:13); "he is merciful and gracious, slow to anger, [and] abundant in goodness" (*Lectures*, 3:14); "he is a God of truth and cannot lie" (*Lectures*, 3:16); and, finally, "he is love" (*Lectures*, 3:18).

A renowned Christian authority observed that "the more unsavory the characters, the more at ease they seemed to feel around Jesus." This scholar then posed a provocative question to church-going individuals: "Why don't sinners like being around us? . . . Somehow we have created a community of respectability. . . . How did Jesus, the only perfect person in history, manage to attract the notoriously imperfect? And what keeps us from following his steps today?" (Phillip Yancey, *The Jesus I Never Knew*, 147–48). Christ sees and understands the inherent value and limitless potential of raw clay. The miraculous transformation that occurred in the Samaritan woman—and each of us when we find God— is only possible with these timeless attributes of the all-wise and loving Potter and our sincere faith in Him.

Other characteristics of unworked clay describe our role as exemplified by this Samaritan woman. Raw clay contains limitless potential to form masterful creations reflecting the finest workmanship. In contrast to other sculpting materials, clay responds easily to the touch and retains even the minutest detail, such as a thumbprint. Each detail imprinted in raw clay can be changed innumerable times until the potter is satisfied and declares the vessel complete.

Like each of us, the Samaritan woman bore the

Clay responds easily to the touch and retains even the minutest detail, such as a thumbprint.

PHOTO BY BRIAN CHRISTENSEN

detailed imprint of her divine parentage. Jesus alluded to such in His teachings to the Jewish leaders. A group of Pharisees and Herodians, attempting to trap Jesus with their cunning questions, asked: "What thinkest thou? Is it lawful to give tribute unto Caesar, or not?" Jesus drew their attention to Tiberius's image engraved in a Roman coin and responded, "Render . . . unto Caesar the things which are Caesar's; and unto God the things that are God's" (Matthew 22:17, 21). From this perspective, if the coin belongs to Caesar because it bears his image, what belongs to God? Where is God's image engraved? Each of us reflects God's likeness because we were created in His image. Give to Caesar and the world what they so cherish, and give ourselves to God. He cares about our souls, not about our possessions.

"Every human soul is stamped with the image and superscription of God," Elder James E. Talmage explained, "however blurred and indistinct the line may have become through the corrosion or attrition of sin; and as unto Caesar should be rendered the coins upon which his effigy appeared, so unto God should be given the souls that bear His image. Render unto the world the stamped pieces that are made legally current by the insignia of worldly powers, and give unto God and His service, yourselves—the divine mintage of His eternal realm" (*Jesus the Christ*, 546–47).

In the metaphor of the Potter, the Lord's handiwork and detail in the clay is an enduring reminder that He formed us and that we will "not be forgotten of [Him]" (Isaiah 44:21).

The Samaritan woman was likewise impressionable, being open to new revelation, while at the same time retaining details of truths passed down for generations. Throughout centuries of apostate influence, Samaritans retained a foundational understanding of a Redeemer. They anticipated the coming of a messianic figure, called the *Taheb* (meaning "restorer"), suggesting one who would restore the Samaritans to both the legitimate worship of God and their rightful place in the house of Israel. Additional descriptions of this messiah were identified from revelations in the first five books of the Old Testament. These records, known as the Pentateuch, Torah, or Books of Moses, were the only scripture accepted by the Samaritans.

Most notable in Samaritan belief is the Deuteronomy prophecy that the Messiah would be a prophet like Moses. Speaking to Moses, God said, "I will raise them up a Prophet from among their brethren, like unto thee, and will put my words in his mouth; and he shall speak unto them all that I shall command him" (Deuteronomy 18:18). The Book of Mormon clarifies that this "Prophet like unto Moses" is Jesus Christ (See 1 Nephi 22:20–21; 3 Nephi 20:23). By retaining these basic truths, the Samaritan woman was being prepared to receive the greatest truth of all. As remarkable as it may initially appear, this woman is the first person mentioned in the Gospels to hear Jesus identify Himself as the Messiah. But that is at the end of the story. She was yet unworked clay when she first encountered Him. How did she come to receive such a profound blessing?

THREE

Preparing the Clay

Like us and the Samaritan woman, clay has weaknesses. Initially clay is unresponsive to the potter's touch, requiring at least three preparatory treatments before it can be shaped. In coming to earth, we inherited a fallen nature which is undisciplined and at odds with the vision of the Potter. We tend toward the course of least resistance, a path that always leads away from Him. Much like raw clay, we must submit to divine treatments if we are to achieve our full potential.

ADDING WATER TO THE CLAY

To make anything of a lump of clay, first, the potter must add water, a simple element but one with vital properties. Water brings the clay to life. Similarly, the symbolic living water we receive from the Savior is as essential to our progress as physical water is to the clay's malleability and usefulness. For example, it is easier to sit as a lump of clay in the comfort and predictability of our chapels talking about gospel principles than to get out into the "street full of splendid strangers" (G. K. Chesterton, *Orthodoxy*, 20–21; also quoted by Neal A. Maxwell, *Ensign*, May 1999, 23) and put those teachings to the test. Actual application of gospel truths brings our testimonies to life. At this stage we note that not only must we receive this living water, but that in our fallen and resistant state, Christ personally brings it to us. In evidence of His condescension, the Savior meets us where we are to deliver His essential treatment.

The woman at the well received it. Jesus came to where He would certainly encounter her, traveling right through the middle of Samaria rather than taking the alternate route. He also met her before she had received an introduction through either His teachings or His miracles. Furthermore, He made no initial

The Savior provides us with living water, which is as essential to our progress as physical water is to clay's malleability and usefulness.

PHOTO BY BRIAN CHRISTENSEN

requirement that she be living in a particular way. Through both His words and His actions, Jesus convincingly taught, "I am not come to call the righteous, but sinners to repentance" (Matthew 9:13). But the woman at the well knew none of this. She saw only a thirsty man sitting on the well. He had none of the equipment necessary to draw water to quench His thirst so He asked the woman for a drink. Perhaps from His dialect or from the weave of His clothing, the woman recognized that the man was a Jew.

When she addressed Him, her greeting was not only without any evidence of respect but filled with awareness of the animosity that separated her people from His. "How is it that thou, being a Jew, askest drink of me, which am a woman of Samaria? for the Jews have no dealings with the Samaritans" (John 4:9). Clearly the woman was on her home turf. The Jewish stranger was the one who was out of place. Initially, they did not communicate on the same level. In the metaphor of the clay, she was unresponsive to His touch. But, just as He spoke with this woman, the Savior can speak in whatever language we can understand.

She came to the well seeking water that sustains mortal life. He offered her something better. He offered living water that sustains eternal life. Jesus said to her: "If thou knewest the gift of God, and who it is that saith to thee, Give me to drink; thou wouldest have asked of him, and he would have given thee living water" (John 4:10). As yet, the woman had no idea that she was conversing with the one man who would selflessly suffer to make this miraculous living water obtainable. She didn't yet realize the One she was facing had the power to give her eternal life.

Her response shows, however, that she was gaining respect for the man and an interest in His proffered gift. For the first time she addressed him as "kyrie," translated from the Greek as "sir" or "lord." Beginning in verse 11, we read: "Sir, thou hast nothing to draw with, and the well is deep: from whence then hast thou that living water? Art thou greater than our father Jacob, which gave us the well?" (John 4:11–12).

In His answer, Jesus emphasized that the water He offered was not at all like the water in that well. No rope or leather bucket was necessary for His promised water. He alone supplies the gift. In reference to the water in Jacob's well, Jesus said, "Whosoever drinketh of this water shall thirst again: But whosoever drinketh of the water that I shall give him shall never thirst; but the water that I shall give him shall be in him a well of water springing up into everlasting life" (John 4:13–14).

I'm certain that I don't understand all that is entailed in the Savior's gift of living water. Surely it must include complete forgiveness, inner peace, personal revelation, and teachings that come through the witness of the Spirit and guide us back to God's presence. Scripture describes the blessings of living water in a variety of contexts. To Joseph Smith, the Lord revealed, "unto him that keepeth my commandments I will give the mysteries of my kingdom, and the same shall be in him a well of living water, springing up unto everlasting life" (D&C 63:23). The prophet Jeremiah chastened Israel for forsaking God, who is "the fountain of living waters" (Jeremiah 2:13). In a dream, the prophet Lehi saw an iron rod leading to "the fountain of living waters, or to the tree of life; which waters are a representation of the love of God" that was given because of the condescension of God (see 1 Nephi 11:25–26). Finally, Moroni was commanded to write to those of the latter days "that evil may be done away, . . . that they may be persuaded to do good continually, that they may come unto the fountain of all righteousness and be saved" (Ether 8:26).

Most assuredly, the woman of Samaria was standing on sacred ground as the Redeemer of the world offered her knowledge by the Spirit and the ultimate promise of eternal life. She quickly responded to the stranger's explanation of living water. Her interest in the gift was deepening and the awe she had for this man was increasing. "Sir," she petitioned, "give me this water, that I thirst not, neither come hither to draw" (John 4:15).

But one wonders what initially motivated her fascination. Was she drawn by the thought of escaping the physical labor and social rejection associated with the well or, rather, by some inkling that there was a better life where thirst is eternally quenched? Was the woman beginning to see that there was hope—real hope—in her world so full of misery? In our metaphor, this ever-lasting water brings the clay to life. When applied to the Samaritan woman, as the message of salvation, ever-lasting water keeps our hopes and faith in Christ alive and is essential to our ability to be shaped by divine influence. In addition, the Potter's gift of living water prepares us for the remaining treatments.

These final two treatments to prepare the clay occur in tandem. First, the potter must dry out the clay while kneading it to eliminate air pockets and second, the potter must remove any and all impurities. In ancient times, the clay was even trodden underfoot to smooth it into a form of paste (see Isaiah 41:25). The potter's kneading can be likened to disappointments and challenges we experience in life as our weaknesses become apparent. Removing the impurities is symbolic of repentance. These treatments are not intended to destroy but to refine and bring about increased wisdom and perspective.

KNEADING THE CLAY

In 1855, Elder Wilford Woodruff told the Saints to trust the hands of the Potter, particularly during times of hardship. He explained, "The chastisements we have had from time to time have been for our good, and are essential to learn wisdom, and carry us through a school of experience we never could have passed through without. I hope, then, that we may learn from the experience we have had to be faithful, and humble, and be passive in the hands of God, and do His commandments" (*Journal of Discourses*, 2:198).

Much like clay that is improved through kneading, the apostle Paul discovered that blessings such as humility come only through hardships. "And lest I should be exalted above measure through the abundance of the revelations," he wrote, "there was given to me a thorn in the flesh, the messenger of Satan to buffet me, lest I should be exalted above measure"

Kneading the clay, in our comparison, is similar to the Savior's refining power as He "kneads" us by revealing our weaknesses and guiding us through trials and challenges in life.

PHOTO BY BRIAN CHRISTENSEN

(2 Corinthians 12:7). The lump of raw clay known as Saul of Tarsus became the masterpiece known as Paul the Apostle when he accepted the refining influence of kneading.

President John Taylor understood the role of adversity in preparing us to return to God. He taught, "It is necessary that we pass through certain ordeals, and that we be tried. But why is it that we should be tried? . . . I heard the Prophet Joseph say, in speaking to the Twelve on one occasion: 'You will have all kinds of trials to pass through. And it is quite as necessary for you to be tried as it was for Abraham and other men of God, and (said he) God will feel after you, and He will take hold of you and wrench your very heart strings, and if you cannot stand it you will not be fit for an inheritance in the Celestial Kingdom of God'" (*Journal of Discourses,* 24:197).

Sometimes I think we expect that our lives will be free from hardship, suffering, and pain if we just continue to pay our tithing, read our scriptures, and do our visiting and home teaching—*most* of the time. When in this mindset, we like to focus on scripture passages that proclaim God's love and concern for us, concluding that He will therefore protect us from any discomfort or distress if we are at least *trying* to keep His commandments. Then we are surprised when sudden bad health precludes long-planned missionary service at retirement, or tragedy hits the most stalwart family in the ward, or marriage continues to elude us.

In times when challenges surface, we may be wise to also notice scriptures where the Lord says, "Whom I love I also chasten" (D&C 95:1); and "My people must be tried in all things, that they may be prepared to receive the glory that I have for them, even the glory of Zion; and he that will not bear chastisement is not worthy of my kingdom" (D&C 136:31). Remember that the Savior came to "heal" broken hearts, not to prevent them from breaking (Luke 4:18). As one meaning of the word *chaste* is *pure*, to *chasten* also means to *purify*.

President James E. Faust cautioned about losing the will to continue when we conclude that others are exempt from suffering such wrenching trials as we have endured. He taught, "Many members, in drinking of the bitter cup that has come to them, wrongfully think that this cup passes by others. . . . Every soul has some bitterness to swallow. Parents having a child who loses his way come to know a sorrow that defies description. A woman whose husband is cruel or insensitive can have her heart broken every day. Members who do not marry may suffer sorrow and disappointment. Having drunk the bitter cup, however, there comes a time when one must accept the situation as it is and reach upward and outward" ("A Second Birth," *Ensign*, June 1998, 2).

Kneading vastly improves flexibility and comprehension. Much of life's wisdom and meaning are revealed only after one graciously endures life's irony and seeming injustice. After a trial of our faith is past, choosing gratitude rather than resentment produces power to discern God's awareness and plan for us.

CLEANSING THE CLAY

In addition to kneading, the clay must be purified before it is shaped. During the kneading process, the potter often notices stones and other foreign objects mixed in with the clay. These impurities are removed by running a wire through the clay as the final preparation before shaping.

Each of us is responsible to willingly deny ourselves of impure thoughts and actions by pursuing the course of repentance. President Brigham Young identified this gospel application in the clay metaphor when he taught, "It is *my* business to . . . use the wire to draw from the lump any material that would obstruct the potter from preparing a vessel unto honor" (*Journal of Discourses,* 4:23; emphasis added). In our analogy, we exercise agency in response to the Potter's offering, reminding us that our role is not a passive one. Through the process of repentance, including confessing and forsaking our sins, we do our part to become pure and receptive in the hands of the Potter.

At the same time, agency allows us to reject Christ's gift of repentance. Our natural tendency is to cling all the more to a weakness when the Potter attempts to eradicate it. In our limited perspective, we fail to detect the harm our resistance creates and the influence

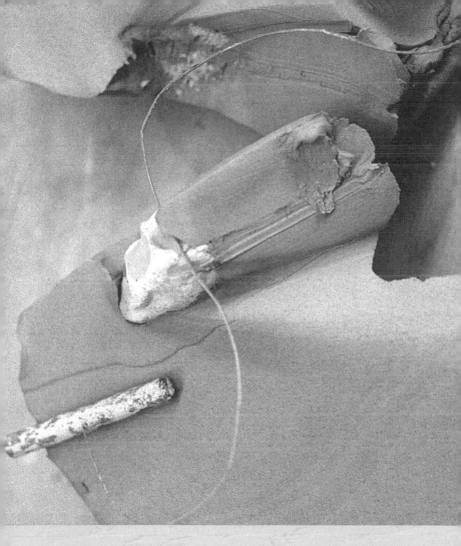

A prepared lump of clay is cleansed by running a wire through it. Similarly, we must willingly deny ourselves of impure thoughts and actions by pursuing the course of repentance.

PHOTO BY BRIAN CHRISTENSEN

wielded by our fears. By relinquishing a stumbling block
to the Lord, we may fear that we are losing the very step
necessary to reach our dreams. We may fear loss of
opportunity, loss of identity, and loss of potential.
Somehow we imagine that God may not love us enough
nor allow us sufficient power to control our lives.

Fortunately for the distrustful among us, the
Savior's enabling power extends to sustain us through
such fears. Through His offering of repentance and forgiveness, the Savior leads us to recognize our weaknesses. By accepting His priceless gift, we are given
strength and wisdom to confront personal sins, short-
comings, and weaknesses that prevented us from wholly
partaking of His supernal gift in the past.

The Samaritan woman encountered the same
opportunity. I think it is instructive that Jesus didn't
begin His conversation with her by pointing out what
she needed to change in order to be accepted by Him.
Rather, He began by helping her see that He had a gift
that was better than anything she had ever experienced. When her problematic lifestyle was finally

brought to light, the Samaritan woman wasn't offended, but reverenced Him even more. "Go, call thy husband," Jesus invited, "and come hither" (John 4:16). She coyly answered, "I have no husband" (v. 17). Notice that initially Jesus even complimented her for telling the truth before spelling out her full story: "Thou hast well said, . . . for thou hast had five husbands; and he whom thou now hast is not thy husband" (John 4:17–18). "Sir," she immediately replied, "I perceive that thou art a prophet" (John 4:19). Again we wonder, "How did Jesus, the only perfect person in history, manage to attract the notoriously imperfect?"

By following the Savior's approach to the woman, we discover that He met her not only where she was physically but also spiritually. He knew that she was looking for a messiah who was a "prophet like unto Moses." As a result of this interchange, Jesus' distinctive and divine identity began to become apparent to her.

Her misconceptions, however, first needed to be removed. Remembering that He was a Jew and she a

Samaritan, she protested, "Our fathers worshipped in this mountain [meaning Mount Gerizim]; and ye say, that in Jerusalem is the place where men ought to worship" (John 4:20). In the seventh century B.C., King Hezekiah forbade temple worship everywhere outside of Jerusalem to curtail apostasy among the Israelites. At the time when Jesus conversed with the woman at the well, the Jews were still adamant about centralized temple worship in Jerusalem. Again, the Samaritans were excluded.

When He said, "The hour cometh, when ye shall neither in this mountain, nor yet at Jerusalem, worship the Father" (John 4:21), Jesus alluded to the fact that the temple in Jerusalem would be destroyed just as the Samaritan temple on Mt. Gerizim had been. He wanted her to understand that specific location is not what is essential to worship, particularly when that location is not founded on truth. Of essential importance, however, is who and how we worship. Incorrect information about the object of our worship and how we worship will assuredly prevent true worship. To correct aspects of Samaritan messianic expectation, Jesus therefore added detail concerning their anticipated "prophet's" mortal origins.

"Ye worship ye know not what: we know what we worship: for salvation is of the Jews" (John 4:22). In contrasting Jewish expectations for a Messiah and knowledge of God to Samaritan worship, Jesus here declared Jewish worship to be better informed. First, rather than restricting prophecy to the writings of Moses as the Samaritans had done, the Jews preserved access to all the holy prophets (see Romans 3:1–2) thereby greatly expanding gospel understanding and knowledge of the Messiah. Furthermore, as one biblical scholar explained it, "the promised deliverer of all Israel (Jews and Samaritans alike) was to come from the tribe of Judah, as even the Samaritan Bible foretold (Gen. 49:10); it was therefore from the Jews—the descendants of Judah—that salvation was to proceed for Israel and the world in general" (F. F. Bruce, *The Gospel of John*, 110).

Regardless of generational conflicts between Jews

and Samaritans, perpetuated in part by the selfishness and arrogance of the Jews, Jesus required the woman at the well to let go of her ethnocentric bias if she would ever discover the anticipated Messiah. If she would receive salvation, she had to acknowledge that more than the Samaritans are included in the infinite mission of the Messiah. Likewise, if we would taste the full sweetness of God's love, we must also conclude that surely salvation has come through the Jews!

Water, kneading, and cleansing are essential to bring us to life. But if faith in Christ is to endure, it must be active. Such faith requires continually flowing living water, return kneadings—even when we think we've suffered them all—and daily inventory to detect and remove impurities. After being born again, how easy it is to slide into complacency and reduce spiritual life to nothing but routine. If we will live abundantly, these preparatory treatments will likely continue throughout our lives.

FOUR

Centering the Clay

Now that the clay is pliable and free from debris, the potter is ready to anchor the clay wedge onto a wheel. In a sure and confident manner, the potter presses the clay up and down until it is centered on the wheel from the edges to the very core. Of critical importance, the clay must be completely centered or it can never respond to the directives of the potter and be formed into a vessel of honor. When the clay doesn't deviate to the left or to the right, the potter knows it is centered. President Heber C. Kimball, a potter by trade, taught, "What makes the clay snap? Because it wants its own way; and you cannot be happy unless you submit to the laws of God, and to the principles of His government" (*Journal of Discourses*, 2:154).

To be molded into a perfect vessel, the clay must be placed on the potter's wheel and pulled up and pushed down continuously until it is perfectly centered. If the clay is not centered, it can never respond to the directives of the potter and be formed into a vessel of honor.

PHOTO BY BRIAN CHRISTENSEN

The Lord's caution that we cannot serve two masters (see Matthew 6:24) is not restricted to choosing between the extremes of good and evil. More frequently, we must decipher God's desires for us from our own worldly pursuits. C. S. Lewis described the tension created when we try to satisfy these two masters. "The terrible thing," he wrote, "the almost impossible thing, is to hand over your whole self—all your wishes and precautions—to Christ. But it is far easier than what we are all trying to do instead. For what we are trying to do is to remain what we call 'ourselves,' to keep personal happiness as our great aim in life, and yet at the same time be 'good.' We are all trying to let our mind and heart go their own way—centered on money or pleasure or ambition—and hoping, in spite of this, to behave honestly and chastely and humbly. And that is exactly what Christ warned us you could not do. . . .

"When He said, 'Be perfect,' He meant it. He meant that we must go in for the full treatment. It is hard; but the sort of compromise we are all hankering after is harder—in fact, it is impossible. It may be hard for an egg to turn into a bird: it would be a jolly sight harder for it to learn to fly while remaining an egg. We are like eggs at present. And you cannot go on indefinitely being just an ordinary, decent egg. We must be hatched or go bad" (*Mere Christianity*, 168–69).

True centeredness requires an eye single to God's glory (see D&C 88:67) because solid conversion to the Lord is the only accurate road map and the only true anchor. We have no need to fear then, because we are centered on the only unshakeable foundation (see Helaman 5:12).

Recall Peter when he walked on water. Far from lacking faith, he initiated the suggestion to step out of a rocking boat in the midst of stormy darkness and walk in the direction of the voice inviting him to "come." President Howard W. Hunter explained the source of Peter's success on the water and why that success faded. He said, "while [Peter's] eyes were fixed upon the Lord, the wind might toss his hair and the spray might drench his robes, but all was well. Only when with wavering faith he removed his glance from the Master to look at the furious waves and the black gulf beneath him, only then did he begin to sink. . . . (adapted from Farrar, *The Life of Christ,* pp. 310–13; see Matt. 14:22–33)" ("The Beacon in the Harbor of Peace," *Ensign,* November 1992, 19).

As we become "centered" on the wheel of the Potter or fix our eyes on Jesus, as President Hunter taught, we too can walk successfully over what one writer called the "swelling waves of disbelief" and remain "unterrified amid the rising winds of doubt" (Frederic W. Farrar, *The Life of Christ,* 313). Like Peter, we will believe the Savior when he says, "Be of good cheer; it is I; be not afraid" (Matthew 14:27). Once we are centered in Him, right to our very core, He enables us to perform beyond our natural abilities. That enabling power includes the ability to recognize the true Messiah and thereby willingly submit our will to His.

Scripture consistently teaches that there is only one way to recognize Jesus as the Savior and Redeemer. The apostle Paul identified the way as clearly as any: "No man can say that Jesus is the Lord, but by the Holy

Ghost" (1 Corinthians 12:3; see also *Teachings of the Prophet Joseph Smith*, 223). One would therefore expect the Holy Ghost to be present when Christ encountered the Samaritan woman. In this the narrative does not disappoint. Christ began to teach the woman to understand His message by the Spirit with this introduction: "The hour cometh, and now is . . ." (John 4:23), suggesting both a future and present application. Again we see the reminder that the way to discover the Lord is the same in any era. Christ created an environment that enabled the Samaritan woman to learn this truth when He explained, "True worshippers shall worship the Father in spirit and in truth: for the Father seeketh such to worship him. For unto such hath God promised his Spirit. And they who worship him, must worship in spirit and in truth (JST John 4:23–24).

Learning in spirit and in truth necessitates the tutelage of the Holy Ghost. His mission is not to speak of himself, but to bear witness of Christ and guide us to "all truth" (John 16:13). That is precisely what the Holy Ghost did for the woman at the well. She carefully listened to Jesus, but it was the Holy Ghost who wove the messianic thread throughout the Savior's teachings. Once taught by the Spirit, she began to put it all together and professed, "I know that Messias cometh, which is called Christ: when he is come, he will tell us all things" (John 4:25). In a sense, like Peter, she took the first step out of the boat and tested her faith.

Then, and only then, Jesus unequivocally declared Himself to be the Messiah. The King James translation records the Savior's response in verse 26 as: "I that speak unto thee am *he*," with the "he" in italics. Italics are used in that translation to indicate words the translators added to the manuscript when clarification was deemed necessary. We are subsequently invited to consider the verse without the italicized word if the result elucidates greater insight. In this case, I believe it does.

One of the Lord's titles is "Jehovah," translated "I Am," as in The Always Existing One. In his gospel, John often recorded statements where Jesus bore witness of himself as the great "I Am." In this verse, if we remove the italicized "he," the Savior confirms His identity to the Samaritan woman by saying, "I Am speaketh unto thee." Through the whisperings of the Spirit and the confirming witness of the Savior, she came to recognize the Savior for herself. Her testimony of the Messiah was at the same time both sure and very personal.

There is only one way to become balanced on the wheel, only one force that stabilizes us when we tip. Christ is the only constant, the only true center. "Many people try to change themselves spiritually," wrote Baptist pastor Dr. Charles Stanley, "and they inevitably come to the same sad conclusion: 'I can't do it by myself.' Only Jesus Christ can cleanse and change a human heart. Only the Holy Spirit, sent by Christ to dwell in us, can guide our decision making, soften our hearts, and trigger our conscience so that we will make choices and initiate Christlike responses. We must never forget—we are the clay. He is the potter!" (*The Blessings of Brokenness*, 39–40).

FIVE

Shaping the Vessel

After the clay is cleansed, pliable, and centered on the wheel, the potter is able to form and shape it into the vessel he has envisioned. During this stage of creation, the potter does not concentrate on the outward appearance of the vessel. Of much greater importance is the inner space. The potter knows that the form of the inner chamber determines the appearance of the exterior. President Ezra Taft Benson spoke of the importance of cleansing the inner vessel, beginning first with ourselves, then our families, and finally with the Church as a whole (see "Cleansing the Inner Vessel," *Ensign,* May 1986, 4–6; see also Alma 60:23).

Society and the world hold a magnifying glass to our outward appearance: the style of our clothing, the

The form of the inner chamber determines the appearance of the exterior of the vessel.

strength of our GPA, the size of our home, the price of our car. In contrast, "the LORD seeth not as man seeth; for man looketh on the outward appearance, but the Lord looketh on the heart" (1 Samuel 16:7). But a bad hair day is much easier to repair than repentance for a serious offense. And so we focus on visual variables rather than on the inconspicuous constants. What a fallacy to think that just because we get a grade change, a new hair style, some plastic surgery, or a remodeled room that we will be better and happier people. Happiness is never found in variableness. In the end, the only things that matter are the constants.

That which comes from the inside, from the heart, reveals our true level of goodness. Our outward appearance merely reflects those desires (see Mark 7:15–23). Much more than what is preached from the pulpit, the apostle Paul taught that we, as individuals and collective members, can be the best epistles of Christ, not written "with ink" or "in tables of stone," but with "the Spirit" when we have internalized Christ in the "fleshy tables of the heart" (2 Corinthians 3:3).

Jesus was more interested in the Samaritan woman's heart than in her current lifestyle. After the Spirit educated the desires of her heart, the direction of her daily life naturally followed. Her change would not be born of a yearning to be accepted by her neighbors but out of love and faith in God. Empowered by faith in and a testimony of Jesus Christ, she would be given the wisdom and strength to take herself out of the dismal downward spiral her life had assumed. "Preach unto them repentance," Alma advised his son Helaman. "Teach them to withstand every temptation of the devil, with their faith on the Lord Jesus Christ" (Alma 37:33). We do not know what earlier spiritual stirrings the woman may have experienced to prod her onto the path of repentance. We know only that this time, as she faced this Jewish stranger at the village well, she made the connection and trusted the witness.

Not all clay vessels assume the potter's desired shape the first time on the potter's wheel; some become marred. President Heber C. Kimball explained that pots are ruined when "they are not contented with the shape the potter has given them, but straightway put themselves into a shape to please themselves; therefore they are beyond understanding what God designs, and they destroy themselves by the power of their own agency" (*Journal of Discourses,* 2:152). The Lord described such individuals as those who "seek not the Lord to establish his righteousness, but every man walketh in his own way, and after the image of his own god, whose image is in the likeness of the world, and whose substance is that of an idol" (D&C 1:16).

This is what Jeremiah meant when he said, "Arise, and go down to the potter's house, and there I will cause thee to hear my words. Then I went down to the potter's house, and, behold, he wrought a work on the wheels. And the vessel that he made of clay was marred in the hand of the potter: so he made it again another vessel, as seemed good to the potter to make it. Then the word of the Lord came to me, saying, O house of Israel, cannot I do with you as this potter? saith the Lord. Behold, as the clay is in the potter's hand, so are ye in mine hand, O house of Israel" (Jeremiah 18:2–6).

Similarly, the apostle Paul referred to our varied responses to Christ: "Hath not the potter power over the clay, of the same lump to make one vessel unto honour, and another unto dishonour?" (Romans 9:21).

All is not lost, however, for those who contend against the Master Potter. As Heber C. Kimball described in a meeting with the Quorum of the Twelve in 1841, marred clay is "cut off the wheel and then thrown back again into the mill, to go into the next batch" (in Joseph Smith, *History of the Church*, 4:478). Thus, clay is given another chance to be obedient and pliable in the hands of the potter. Even so, through sincere repentance individuals can start again—surrender, submit, and make themselves available and accessible to the Lord, willing to hear His word and follow His direction. We can yet become honorable vessels to Him, worthy to stand as witnesses of His name to others.

The woman at the well was ready to start again. This time, she possessed sufficient faith to surrender and submit, gladly willing to relinquish her problem past. As soon as she received the message from the

Remnants of clay that have been worked and reworked are symbolic of our own chance to repent and at last become obedient and pliable in the hands of the Potter.

PHOTO BY BRIAN CHRISTENSEN

Spirit and the confirmation from the Messiah, she "left her waterpot, and went her way into the city, and saith to the men, Come, see a man, which told me all things that ever I did: is not this the Christ?" (John 4:28–29). Perhaps the waterpot signifies the woman's former life—including her dependence on a sinful world in order to survive. He who is both the living water and the giver of the water eliminates our dependence on the world's programs and success formulas. One drinks living water; one does not carry it. Therefore, a waterpot is not needed.

Now converted, the Samaritan woman's greatest desire was to share the good news with everyone in her village. She forgot about herself, her past, and her reputation. No doubt some of those who believed her message were individuals who had previously mistreated her. Furthermore, notice that she used an approach similar to the Savior's to introduce the truth to her neighbors. She met them where they were both physically and spiritually. She went to them in the city and witnessed that she had found that "prophet, like unto Moses." "Come," she invited, "see a man, which told me all things that ever I did: is not this the Christ?" (John 4:29).

When a vessel is shaped around the foundation of Christ, it becomes serviceable to the Lord, even an extension of Him. We should then not be surprised to remember the Redeemer when we use the vessel rather than the fine qualities of the clay. For example, as a result of the Samaritan woman's testimony, many came to worship the true God. Initially, they believed because of the "saying of the woman." But after having Jesus as a guest in their village for two days, they knew by the Spirit. These new Samaritan converts proclaimed to the woman, "Now we believe, not because of thy saying: for we have heard him ourselves, and know that this is indeed the Christ, the Saviour of the world" (John 4:42).

At a time when few Jews knew the true identity of Jesus, a little village in Samaria proclaimed the truth of truths, the declaration of declarations: "this is indeed the Christ, the Saviour of the world." Like Andrew, brother of Simon Peter, they could proclaim with delight, "We have found the Messia[h]" (John 1:41).

SIX

Entrusting Ourselves to the Potter

Throughout the clay-forming process, agency is present. A good potter respects the clay by not moving it faster than it can endure and by never vigorously forcing it into a shape. With a combination of pinching and pulling movements, adding water constantly to keep the clay flexible and alive, the potter leads the vessel to its proper form. A good potter can sense unique tendencies within each wedge of clay that, when followed, lead to the creation of a different vessel every time.

Despite the promise of a glorious transformation, we often balk at the thought of entrusting ourselves to the

Tendencies in the clay lead the potter to create a different vessel each time a lump is placed upon his wheel. Likewise, unique human tendencies lead the Master Potter to shape and refine us individually, each time creating a different human vessel.

POTTERY AND PHOTOS BY BRIAN CHRISTENSEN

Master Potter's vision and power. Such a counterintuitive reaction may occur for a variety of reasons. I will discuss three such reasons.

First, some hesitate to trust the Potter out of fear. We fear responsibility that could result in failure. We fear trying something new, knowing that it will invite almost certain pain. We may fear that we are doing things wrong out of ignorance and have not the skills to learn the better way. This lack of confidence includes doubting our ability to commune with and understand the direction of the Spirit. Similarly, we may fear that God does not care so much about our mundane lives. Such fears create feelings of profound loneliness. Imagine the intense feelings of vulnerability in the woman of Samaria as she discovered that this stranger at the well knew more about herself than did she. But she trusted. The metaphor of the Potter and the clay reminds us that we cannot succeed alone. The Potter must be with us; and most assuredly, He desires to guide us.

Elder Henry D. Moyle taught the necessity of recognizing promptings from the Spirit if we are to trust the vision the Potter sees for each of us. "Without . . . [the] power of the Holy Ghost," he taught, "you and I would not be able to become submissive to the will of our Heavenly Father. We would not know what his will is, except by the gift and power of the Holy Ghost. Then when we know what his will is, we must be as clay in the hands of the potter to permit our lives to be molded in the pattern that the Savior of mankind set for us" (in Conference Report, April 1950, 148).

Some of us would rather trust other mortals to make decisions for us because if things don't work out as expected, we have someone to blame besides ourselves. If we don't know how to be alone with ourselves and our thoughts, we likely will miss the subtle, inward direction of the Spirit. Our lives can become so filled with schedules, deadlines, social events, and noise that the silence and stillness essential to inspiration seem uncomfortable to us.

During a time of great persecution by Missouri mobs, the Savior taught Joseph Smith, "Be still and know that I am God" (D&C 101:16). Both King

Mosiah and the high priest Alma knew the heartache of children who strayed. The scriptures do not report that they consulted and commiserated with each other, though they may have done so. Instead, they turned to God for answers. When we consciously create an environment where the Spirit can accompany our musings and concerns, faith in the Lord's promises is nourished and fortified. Wisdom to respond to life's threats is given in such a way as to reinforce that the Lord is in control. Achieving this eternal perspective, we can declare with reverent confidence: "If God be for us, who can be against us?" (Romans 8:31).

Others resist submitting to the Lord for a second reason. Individuals who have been abused, mistreated, or denied personal freedom by someone they loved and trusted in the past and who wielded earthly power may conclude that God in His infinite power will treat them in a similar manner. Fears of being vulnerable again, as well as the possible consequences, can cause us to put up barriers and defenses. When our trust has been violated by another, we can become convinced that someone else who appears to love us today may only be scheming to take advantage of our trust tomorrow. But our Master Potter is a perfect being whom we can fully and forever trust. "The Lord has revealed himself and his perfect character, possessing in their fulness all the attributes of love, knowledge, justice, mercy, unchangeableness, power, and every other needful thing, so as to enable the mind of man to place confidence in him without reservation" (Bible Dictionary, "Faith," 669).

Jesus Christ came to earth to "heal the broken-hearted, to preach deliverance to the captives, and recovering of sight to the blind, to set at liberty them that are bruised" (Luke 4:18). We have absolutely no need to fear that the Lord would ever harm or disappoint us. His perfect love will cover and infinitely heal bruises caused by others. We can implicitly trust Him and His tender promises.

Perhaps the greatest stumbling block in entrusting ourselves to the Lord is pride. Pride entices us to think we are doing just fine on our own; we can handle life and therefore need not trouble the Lord with our concerns. In Jeremiah's time, the kingdom of Judah was chastised for not only forsaking the Lord as the "fountain of living waters," but for insisting that they design their own water vessels rather than allow the Lord's handiwork. The result was disastrous. Their vessels, created without the Lord, were totally dysfunctional, described as "broken cisterns, that can hold no water" (Jeremiah 2:13). Like Korihor, the Book of Mormon antichrist, we may assume that we owe our current greatness to our own management and intellect (see Alma 30:17).

Being puffed up with our own sense of competence and skill is indicative of fallen man, wholly without foundation. Consider your own situation in life. How did you arrive at such a status? How many others made sacrifices for you—gave you guidance, advice, moral and financial support? Who served as role models for you? Who simply gave you an opportunity to prove yourself?

Often, while walking across a large university campus,

I am reminded of former generations of students and faculty. The older buildings and walkways on campus were constructed when fewer students were instructed by a smaller faculty and led by a simpler system of administration. Technology, as we utilize it today, would have been unfathomable to students of earlier eras. Yet those students came to college then as eager to learn and hopeful of their potential contribution to the world as most students come today. The older buildings on campus remind me that we are the recipients of the inventions, inspiration, and courageous endeavors of countless former graduates and faculty. We have exponentially more opportunities available to us today because of their sacrifices and contributions. As Isaac Newton wisely noted long ago, "If [we] have seen further [or accomplished more] it is by standing upon the shoulders of Giants" (from a letter to Robert Hooke, 5 February 1675; see also John Bartlett, *Familiar Quotations*, 379).

Beyond the acknowledgement of our fellowman, we are indebted to Jesus Christ. So often we take His sublime gifts without a thought of our dependence on Him. "At first it is natural for a baby to take its mother's milk without knowing its mother," C. S. Lewis wrote. "It is equally natural for us to see the man who helps us without seeing Christ behind him. But we must not remain babies. We must go on to recognise the real Giver. It is madness not to. Because, if we do not, we shall be relying on human beings. And that is going to let us down. The best of them will make mistakes; all of them will die. We must be thankful to all the people who have helped us, we must honour them and love them. But never, never pin your whole faith on any human being: not if he is the best and wisest in the whole world. There are lots of nice things you can do with sand; but do not try building houses on it" (*Mere Christianity*, 163).

The Pharisee Nicodemus provides the warning example of letting pride get in the way of trusting the Lord. His attitude and self-image contrast strikingly with that of the Samaritan woman. I don't think it is coincidental that his story immediately precedes her story in the gospel of John.

Nicodemus was a man—that fact alone would establish him in the upper echelon of Jewish society. The woman at the well was a woman *and* a Samaritan, a double reason to be labeled unclean by the Jews.

He was a Pharisee, well respected, among the best educated, and considered by many to be the master teacher of Israel (John 3:10). By contrast, the woman of Samaria had an unsavory past and would have received no respect in the community. He would have been recognized as a most religious individual. She would be identified with the gravest of sinners.

Nicodemus chose to seek answers from the Lord at night. This way, no one would see a prestigious rabbi conversing with a carpenter from Galilee. On the other hand, her exchange with Jesus occurred at mid-day in the midst of her daily chores.

Nicodemus sought to learn from the Savior after hearing about Him through reputed miracles He had performed in Jerusalem. Additionally, Nicodemus came on his terms, not the Lord's. By contrast, Jesus met the woman where she was, without any show of miracles or previous introduction.

Nicodemus returned to his daily routine, presumably keeping his conversation with Jesus a secret. She left her waterpot behind and spread the good news to all those who would hear her.

With all his power and position and opportunity for learning, Nicodemus couldn't see who stood before him. But the woman at the well, in her humble and demeaning circumstances, saw. Pride in thinking he could progress without the help of the Potter created a barrier to the very knowledge Nicodemus spent his life pursuing.

Perhaps one reason the Savior admonishes us to "become as little children" (Matthew 18:3) is that children are so pliable, free from pride, and receptive to direction from others. A friend reported to a priesthood leader that she overwhelmingly preferred her calling in the Primary to her previous assignment of teaching adults in Sunday School. "I can understand that," the leader responded. "In Primary you still get to work in wet cement." When we refuse to allow the Potter to mold us because of our pride, we cease to accept His living water, and the dry clay is set.

We have frequently heard prophets refer to us as a "chosen generation," reserved to come to earth at this important time. I have wondered what that means. What should we be doing to fulfill our important purpose? Is it to become the best composer? the greatest engineer? a mother who is simultaneously successful at home and in a prestigious career? I don't think so. Such a focus easily blurs the central importance of the Potter while concentrating on our own merits. I am intrigued by the absence of pride expressed in a thought by President Joseph F. Smith:

"To do well those things which God ordained to be the common lot of all man-kind, is the truest greatness. To be a successful father or a successful mother is greater than to be a successful general or a successful statesman. One is universal and eternal greatness, the other is ephemeral. . . . Many are unhappy because they imagine that they should be doing something unusual or something phenomenal. Some people would rather be the blossom of a tree and be admiringly seen than be an enduring part of the tree and live the commonplace life of the tree's existence" (*Gospel Doctrine*, 285–86).

President James E. Faust likewise taught, "It has been said that this church does not necessarily attract great people but more often makes ordinary people great. . . . Any man or woman who enjoys the Master's touch is like potter's clay in his hands. More important than acquiring fame or fortune is being what God wants us to be. Before we came to this earth, we may have been fashioned to do some small good in this life that no one else can do. . . . If God has a work for those with many talents, I believe he also has an important work for those of us who have few" ("Five Loaves and Two Fishes," *Ensign*, May 1994, 4). We cannot proudly chase worldly pursuits with our God-given gifts while we claim we have turned our lives over to God. No man can serve two masters.

Perhaps our greatest mission is to show by the way

we approach each day, each assignment, even in the most challenging times, that we will remain valiant, that we will be solid and steadfast, covenant-honoring individuals. Again, when we let go of pride, the uniquely exquisite vessel with its important mission may go unnoticed, but assuredly it will be hard to miss the Savior and His sacrifice.

Undoubtedly, other reasons to reject the Potter's invitation exist. No matter the reason, however, the result will be the same. Without the tender touch, the mercy, merits, and grace of the Master Potter, we can never become what God envisions for us—to be like Him (see 1 John 3:2). "Be thou humble; and the Lord thy God shall lead thee by the hand, and give thee answer to thy prayers" (D&C 112:10). "Whatever Jesus lays His hands upon lives," taught Elder Howard W. Hunter. "If Jesus lays His hands upon a marriage, it lives. If He is allowed to lay His hands upon a family, it lives" ("Reading the Scriptures," *Ensign*, November 1979, 65).

SEVEN

The Completed Vessel

When the potter is satisfied with the shape and design of the vessel, both inside and out, he fires and glazes it, forever preserving its completeness or perfection. Baked clay tablets, used for writing surfaces in antiquity, are the most resilient records of ancient history because of their ubiquitous use and remarkable preservation through millennia. The same may be said of the Potter's ultimate design for us.

When, at the Final Judgment, we have received our resurrected bodies, we may marvel at the universal gift of resurrection and the remarkable restoration to wholeness that occurs (see Alma 40:23). Most amazing may be that, much like the countless times a wedge of clay may be reworked before it is at last fired and glazed, our resurrected bodies will not reflect any evidence of the number of times we may have been returned to the wheel for re-formation.

For that reason we must remember that the story of the Samaritan woman at the well is not a parable. The event actually happened. The Savior met a Samaritan woman where she was, helped her to see her weaknesses, and created an environment where she could learn His identity through the witness of the Holy Ghost. When filled with this knowledge, she abandoned her sins and became the catalyst that led an entire village to Christ. In other words, the Samaritan woman can receive just as glorious an eternal future as will "our glorious Mother Eve" (D&C 138:39) and Mary, the "most beautiful and fair above all other virgins" (1 Nephi 11:15).

Who knows what dramatic shifts and turns the Samaritan woman must have encountered in life after she received the Messiah's witness. Certainly her glorious outcome was not what she imagined while she walked to the well that day. Likewise, no one can tell us

A completed vessel reveals no evidence of the number of times it may have been returned to the wheel and reworked before it was fired and glazed.

    POTTERY AND PHOTO BY BRIAN CHRISTENSEN

just how our lives will unfold or how to avoid all misfortune. We can design our most-hoped-for life and painstakingly work to achieve it, but, fortunately for you and for me, it will not likely happen as we have planned. We will encounter surprising turns that we never could have anticipated. Some of these are likely the result of the Lord's guiding hand in our lives. Elder Dallin H. Oaks wisely counseled, "Do not rely on planning every event of your life—even every important event. Stand ready to accept the Lord's planning and the agency of others in matters that inevitably affect you. Plan, of course, but fix your planning on personal commitments that will carry you through no matter what happens. Anchor your life to eternal principles, and act upon those principles whatever the circumstances and whatever the actions of others. Then you can await the Lord's timing and be sure of the outcome in eternity" (2001–2002 Devotional Speeches, 192).

Ultimately we can know that the Lord is in control. He is the Master. As a result of being submissive to His will, we have richer, more meaningful lives. We can look back at our pasts and recognize the guidance of the Lord. "As often as thou hast inquired thou hast received instruction of my Spirit," the Lord witnessed. "If it had not been so, thou wouldst not have come to the place where thou art at this time" (D&C 6:14). Why should we question that He will continue to direct us in the future?

President Ezra Taft Benson identified how our mortal life is improved in ten different ways when we submit to the Lord: "Men and women who turn their lives over to God will discover that He can make a lot more out of their lives than they can. He will deepen their joys, expand their vision, quicken their minds, strengthen their muscles, lift their spirits, multiply their blessings, increase their opportunities, comfort their souls, raise up friends, and pour out peace" (*The Teachings of Ezra Taft Benson*, 361).

The truths about the Potter and the clay ring clearer to me now than ever in the past because each year I receive unexpected opportunities with compensating abilities that consistently bear it out. Clearly, my life has not unfolded as that Tremonton teenager imagined. It has been infinitely better and significantly more challenging—with more refining yet to come. I have felt the touch of the Master Potter and His miraculous re-formation. How do I now explain that to today's teenagers who plan to micro-manage life so they can get it all? What words of hope can I communicate to one who has already suffered much loss while standing at the first of life's crossroads? What can I relate to a friend who has sipped everywhere except at the Well and is now dying of thirst? How do I convincingly testify that a righteous desire becomes a major miracle when it comes in the Lord's way, according to His timetable, even when the realization of that desire may be decades away? I doubt I can be very successful in my attempt. Why? Finding God is a personal journey. No one can travel that path for us. If this little book then has any worth, it will be a catalyst for sparking personally meaningful questions while reconfirming the only viable Source for the answers. Satisfying answers come only when we meet Him—alone—at the well.

The woman of Samaria experienced this life-changing discovery. Isn't that the miracle? This woman who doesn't even have a name in our scriptures got it! This woman who would never be a standout in a crowd is known by Jesus. She who has neither title, nor position, nor formal education, nor a stainless past *sees*—she actually sees the thirsty stranger as He truly is, the Savior and Redeemer of the world.

Life-changing revelation came to her—revelation as profound as we find anywhere in scripture. But her conversion was not in the dramatic fashion of Alma the younger or Saul on the road to Damascus. In a quiet and contemplative way, the Samaritan woman received a clear witness while in the midst of doing ordinary housework. If she can recognize the Savior and overcome her hang-ups to follow Him wholeheartedly, certainly there is hope and an invitation for you and me.

Whenever I return to visit the Tremonton First Ward chapel, I still stare and marvel at the mural of Jesus' encounter with the Samaritan woman. She is not only there at church every Sunday, but she is also in many of our temples. Why is she there? She who suffered from spiritual dehydration was offered and received everlasting water. And ever since that day, her story has been a light to any sincere truth-seeker.

She invites all to come unto Christ as she preserves the defining imprint of the Master Potter. She bears witness of the miracle that awaits us when we embark on our personal journey to find God. He loves every lump of clay in His desire to shape us into magnificent vessels. Along with the woman of Samaria, we, too, will be designed, fired, and glazed for all eternity.

Works Cited

2001–2002 Devotional Speeches. Provo: Brigham Young University, 2002.

Bartlett, John. *Familiar Quotations.* 14th ed. Boston: Little, Brown and Company, 1968.

Benson, Ezra Taft. *The Teachings of Ezra Taft Benson.* Salt Lake City: Deseret Book, 1988.

Bruce, F. F. *The Gospel of John.* Grand Rapids, Mich.: Eerdmans, 1983.

Chesterton, G. K. *Orthodoxy.* Garden City, New York: Doubleday, 1959.

Conference Report of The Church of Jesus Christ of Latter-day Saints. Salt Lake City: The Church of Jesus Christ of Latter-day Saints, April 1950.

Ensign. Salt Lake City: The Church of Jesus Christ of Latter-day Saints, 1971–.

Farrar, Frederic W. *The Life of Christ.* New York: E. P. Dutton & Company, 1875.

Journal of Discourses, 26 vols. London: Latter-day Saints' Book Depot, 1854–86.

Lewis, C. S. *Mere Christianity.* New York: Macmillan, 1960.

McConkie, Bruce R. *Mormon Doctrine,* 2d ed. Salt Lake City: Bookcraft, 1966.

Mishnah. Translated by Herbert Danby London: Oxford University, 1933.

Smith, Joseph. *History of The Church of Jesus Christ of Latter-day Saints.* Edited by B. H. Roberts. 7 vols. 2d ed. rev. Salt Lake City: Deseret Book, 1932–51

———. *Lectures on Faith.* Salt Lake City: Deseret Book, 1985.

———. *Teachings of the Prophet Joseph Smith.* Selected by Joseph Fielding Smith. Salt Lake City: Deseret Book, 1976.

Smith, Joseph F. *Gospel Doctrine.* Salt Lake City: Deseret Book, 1977.

Stanley, Charles. *The Blessings of Brokenness.* Grand Rapids, Mich.: Zondervan, 1997.

Talmage, James E. *Jesus the Christ.* Salt Lake City: Deseret Book, 1976.

Yancey, Phillip. *The Jesus I Never Knew.* Grand Rapids, Mich.: Zondervan, 1995.